Lid to the Shadow

Lid to the Shadow

Alexandria Peary

SLOPE EDITIONS

Library of Congress Cataloging-in-Publication Data
Peary, Alexandria, 1970-
    Lid to the shadow / Alexandria Peary.
        p. cm.
    Poems.
    ISBN 978-0-9777698-6-5
    I. Title.
PS3616.E266L53 2011
811'.6--DC22
2010051502

For Michael

For Sophia

For Simone

ACKNOWLEDGMENTS

The author wishes to thank Caroline Knox and Michael Earl Craig for their virtual and telephone conversations (nourishment) about poetry. She also acknowledges her students, including Erin Bachand, Melissa Pettiford, and Sean Rogers, for their ideas about some of the poems in this book. She also thanks the editors at Slope Editions and her designer, Chip Russell, for all of their assistance.

Lastly, the author gratefully acknowledges the editors of the journals in which the following poems first appeared:

Denver Quarterly: "The Cherry Blossoms Were" and "The Logic of Spring"

Gettysburg Review: "How About Daphne"

jubilat: "Orchard in a Flurry"

Literary Imagination: "The Origins of Spring" and "White Orchard"

New American Writing: "The Entrance of Spring," "The Gift," and "Prodigal"

Stand: "Sung"

Tygerburning: "tiny low garden" and "In the courtyard"

Verse: "Title with shadow"

CONTENTS

FOREWORD

I love Alexandria Peary's *Lid To The Shadow.* Most of the new poetry I've been encountering for years, for decades, it seems, is straight gray button-down competent and lethally boring—I read it aware that I will never return to it. The moment I opened Peary's collection, I knew I was in the presence of a mind witty, kind, and somehow preternaturally wise. The wit is magnificently controlled and understated, and emitting, or so it seems to me, qualities which originate in a mind that's taken a few spins around reality and knows something about the wisdom of resignation. The thing is, the book is so much fun, the startling twists and turns in these weirdly tender mock narratives and wry lyric poems fueled by the kind of encounters with what we think of as objective reality (the one in which we are supposedly, all of us, embubbled) that evidently drove the poet to seek an alternative, private and secret world all her own, one infinite as this one—Hart Crane's heartbreaking line comes to mind: *I was promised an improved infancy* . . . But I had no sense of a secret and individual inner world as a form of escape from reality but, on the contrary, just the thing to enhance its beauty, which is basically the beauty of getting to be here, getting to witness the light or the stars when either we or those stars might so easily not be here, not exist at all; important to keep in mind, however, if you ask me, is that this secret world is also a shield against the unendurable horrors of the world. Not a place to hide, you see, but that which enabled her to wade pretty unscathed right into the action, the vast adventure, participation in which means one must first overcome and defeat fear, the justifiable fear of getting out of bed, of dressing and leaving the house! Anyway, I want to say something about style and form themselves:

I perceived right away in her pages a great intensity of effort, of persistence, but mostly of love for the art itself, qualities I think one finds in true writers. True writers being the ones who not only possess a verbal talent but a drive, a desire to work; to work so hard and obsessively that the secrets and incredible complexities of the language itself unfold and reveal ways to write with simplicity and clarity, to dare, that is, to write in such a way that any false step, anything contrived and artificial, is immediately apparent. One obvious reason younger or more inexperienced writers have so often, and with such absurd results, attempted to emulate the masters of obscurity is that if, as a young writer, you can create enough fog, diversions, and obscurities for obscurity's sake, it is impossible to tell whether your have any talent, any real and/or visionary experience of life, or even anything of interest to say. Bluntly, Peary's book is *interesting*. The great poet Donald Justice used that term once with me in correspondence, remarking something to the effect of "how few really interesting books of poetry there are." Once again, staggering simplicity of expression in order to communicate something about a mystery ... it has taken me a long, bitter time to appreciate the depth of Justice's statement. To be "interesting" seemed a fairly pedestrian aspiration, when it came to the poem. I don't feel that way any more. Life is fleeting, every moment is precious, and I don't want to waste any of it reading poetry written by sheep. I want to read language that is mysterious yet starkly clear and possessed of that seemingly effortless and unendingly free and resourceful flow of words that come into the world when a talented mind takes seriously and rejoices in the possibilities available to her at every step when she so clearly works out of a radiant awareness of English prosody. And it doesn't matter whether this comes easily and naturally to the poet or only after she has expended all the energy required to truly pay attention to this essential matter, to be completely awake and alive to the improvisatory possibilities that exist for someone who has understood that the best way to break rules is to first master them. Anyway, I want to give you my personal guarantee that you

XIV

need this book—and will benefit greatly from reading it as well as have a riotously good time. A good deal. Alexandria Peary has opened a door to a marvelous wealth of future poetry, and I am not only curious and excited to see where she goes from here, I am also relieved and grateful to be aware she is out there working on whatever it is she is working on right now. But I almost hope it doesn't come too soon—I know I am going to be living with and wandering around in *this* lovely and powerful collection for a long time.

Franz Wright
November 23, 2010
Waltham, Massachusetts

Lid to the Shadow

One Thousand Years of
Chinese Poetry

When my husband said the other day that poetry was my baby,
I put on oven mitts and took
the temperature of my baby, for a hot-pink chart
had spread over her cheeks,
soon to blossom into cherries
and logic, if not addressed.

My husband was dropping issues in the background,
tissues of Windex and Timex
after making them into paper cranes
in the white shadow where she slept, nestled
inside a vintage Fisher Price toy,
the trough from the school house set
back at Honky Tonk town,
near the Temple of Flying River.

People name their children all sorts of things
these days. I've heard ESPN (pronounced "Es-pen"),
not to mention Apple, September, Moon Unit Diesel, Sickle Root.
I suppose I pushed her out of the same red shadow,
at the same moment. I supposed that two years
was a long time to go without a name, or without fingernails.
And, yes, I suppose that there were a lot of strange things
happening that day under the blossoming cherry tree.

Prodigal

Ovals on a shaking stick
black almonds on a branch
a branch with portals
stands up in the foliage of every day
to the foliage of a long day
which is scrambled and unscrambled
mostly yellow and orange pieces
a camouflage of Tuesday
and Biblical passages
champagne and trash can lids
with small numbers in their dis
continued rims.
This time what is said will stick.
A crack in the family plaid.
A sapling, mere novice,
is held up out of a manhole shadow
by a hand in the bleaching cold

Plaid oil cloth on the table
and the dullard wine bottle,
in the plaster above the table
a drawing of a hole
left by an explosion
inside which is a bottle-green forest
coded pastoral
the place where long ago

the sister left but returned,
and then the olive-green jungle
coded prodigal,
place where the brother left
as the tape of the sky is speeded up.
Exit, robbery, walk-off
escape plan, exile
are ovals in a wood bowl
set on the lid of a shadow,
dish of white portals
from which a stone hand
occasionally sneaks almonds.

Title with shadow

" " are put around a tree which is plaid but smells fruity
and then the white field slides to the right of the poem
in the awkward jump my Royal typewriter makes for a huge tab
to jut from the side as they walk to find the manager
while the whole ½ mile is reeled back in
though the walk back is pleasant, like chewing gum
or chewing on color. In Ugg boots, they traipse around
stepping over white shapes in the white, looking up from
        watching their feet
to discuss the title up at top which doesn't help,
a group of charcoal letters with a steel shadow
ineffectual as a billboard in the middle of nowhere
(perhaps nowhere grew around it). Some people
may be discomforted by walking in a forest inside white
and not knowing which season it is, so an icon of a yellow leaf
falls. They walk by the trees they passed up—
the blaze orange one, "Garage Band," smelling of Johnny Walker,
the one covered in American flags, others smelling like
        "grandma's kitchen,"
"clean air," and the tree that's an open window which they
        almost took,
that row moving jerkily as though on a conveyor belt.
They reach the manager who grumbles about people ripping
        trees off
in the middle of the night, he wants to install a surveillance camera
so sensitive it will respond to the wedge of moon and the most
        poetic moves of leaves

and, indeed, they had seen on their way down how instead
of stumps, there were little gashes in the cardboard
where the staples had been. Everyone needs a title,
for finished books and ones written only for the shelf in oneself.
A title is good for any car. It will make the ride smell better.
Quotation marks around a leaf make it ring like a bell
like this one outside the manager's lean-to. Tired by now, the
    look back
in the middle of the lane, not having a thought,
The title with shadow— cone-less original—
In the white lane, A figure made of sea glass,
Kelp moving in the shadow.

Blossoming Cherry Tree to the Tune of "Frank Lloyd Wright"

I think I was the only person on the tour
of the famous house, the only person
in the three-part fold of the brochure
with the π sign as furniture and the rich
brown carapace of the division sign coffee table,
the music stand, lyre, and the folded screen
of flat gold monks leaving the scene,
quitting, the scene too prissy, needing more
mountain-side explosions, the only person
to notice the deep mahogany ovals
pretending to be shadows in the landscaping
right outside the house
and that they were sending signals
to the enemy, right there beside the paisley ferns
who wear their message openly on their bodies
in rusty-red Braille.

Everyone else was distracted by the dividend
that appears in the steam of the falling water,
the figure of a woman who sometimes turns up
in the pounding of the mist to give advice
about the financial markets, or they were thinking
about the fact that the owners lived in art
every moment of their lives—Mrs.
Zimmerman at eighty fell down a huge flight
of stairs in an art museum, & she made
all her own table linens to match the architect's bricks
and that was a glass that Max Ernst

drank ginger ale out of, gold polka dots,
a go-go dancer, & Welcome to Alaska on it,
set on a curlicue probably carved by Marx.
Everyone was too busy to notice that the landscaping
included dark circles, along with cedar chips.

Ferns of course are among the oldest of plants
much like the out-of-date office equipment
also dragged out of the house
to become part of the lawn design,
rolodexes, dot matrix printers, and a mimeo
graph machine, right beside the wading plants
the neighbor, a Korean war veteran,
carved to hide the shortwave radio equipment
he used to communicate to his son in Vietnam
to hide his basement loss from his sleeping wife,
and it was right then that the pillows started appearing,
bolsters, neck pillows and yard pillows
seat cushions, and full-length body pillows, throw ones too
pillow cases with the sheen of ribbon candy
from an old ballerina, like accepting ancient
candy, lumpy and strange, from an old lady's palm,
like eating the piece of the banister her parents leaned against
at an opera in 1922, taken from a velvet box, like tasting
the scratchy material upholstery of the chair
from the back of a sitting room, like agreeing
to drinks called Grasshopper and Sandy

left on the long insect torso of the table
with foot knobs.

It was my fifth wedding anniversary.
Someone pointed out how much I looked like one of
Eddie Hopper's women on the lawn
as the tail of the tour snapped back to its head
near the rhododendrons.
I sat there in my tennis-white dress &
straw hat made in China and ate a sandwich
to wash out my mouth. I saw someone slip
out of the back door. It may have been one of the flattened monks,
or it may have been the flowering branch
that reached right inside the house
through an opening in one of the sliders
in How Spring Invited Winter into the House.
Or, as I say, water over falling bridge,
Falling water over bridge.

In the courtyard

Some mauve words, some beaded trees
this part of spring overwhelms me,
each planted tree a comparison
done in seed pearls, a version
onto which strips of lilac felt are pressed
then held in place for a few seconds
above a generalized base—
as though created by someone skilled with a glue gun
& the types of detail I'm no good at.
I can't compete: what I've done
stands toward the back of the courtyard near the church wall
a few fuzzy words that I put there several years ago.
That one of the words has turned a shade of ochre
that's hard to come by—that I've been trying to put my hands
    on for years—
purely by chance (plus exposure to a few
back-to-back winters) is most discouraging.

The Entrance of Spring

This part of spring still overwhelms me
3-part, unfolded and leaning on the outside
of the stone and unitarian church
the center panel taken up by a lime green blur,
while everyone is inside at the service
the first sign appears and is tall as the building,
part of a plan that is grudgingly shared with me
that's still no help, I can't follow along

and by then it's the third week in May
and leaning outside the church
is a Tarot card with the kind of cherry tree
that grows inside a math problem,
all fractures and color, that exists in a time
in which great problems are solved
an exactness in art, a tree without longing,
a flowering that others have already got right.
The Paramour to the young men in the Science bldg
Tree with pink sleeves—placed on top of the Origins of Spring,
Seven of Cups—a black wind runs through them.

The Origins of Spring

A diagram becomes a cherry tree
blanks to write in
are that old-looking pink
the same as the index cards
faded with his pencil scrawl
that moment under glass
in which the math and the poem were found
in the pink, the experienced pink

a technical drawing of a tree
bulleted   cherry   blossoming
in a private garden in an old text book
that comes before the famous architect's house
which always reminds me of
water falling outside a long division problem
really, a fancy raised ranch.

A diagram becomes a cherry tree
a bullet on one of the flash cards
scattered on the ground.
I put it in my pocket and tighten the sash
of my paper overcoat

The Logic of Spring

In another poem, called The Logic of Spring,
    a mechanical drawing of a tree
that I've passed a 100 times
    on my way to a different problem.
I glance backwards, and the stack of the day
multiplies, glancing backwards several times,
the dog-eared corner with the graph paper sky of that morning
    and the logic of spring.
Right before I wake, I hear the riposte of mean jays (blue dots
    that drag the pink banners of answers off the tree
with words in gold italic latin)
    from the fog pumped in by the machine
set on my lawn. First thing in the morning,
(page numbers in all the dish rags hanging around the sink)
    I part the buttery curtains
to see beyond the doric columns sitting on my porch & the
    hibiscus twig
that someone has set the stump of such a tree—gray
    smudges and still intact line breaks
with flashing pink splashes—
outside my house while I slept.
Seems unbearably cruel until
I realize that in the flapping fog I finally hear its questions.
Are you so easily distracted
    by pieces of a poem
attached to a tree?
    in which as the situation changes
you catch glimpses of yourself
    a series of emoticons.

Pantoum with Portal

On the crushed blue, bird song
and the budding branches are tubes
sign at the end of a long
Branch, perhaps one of the beatitudes

while the budding branches are tubes
and in the morning there is nothing but creeping
along the Branch, perhaps one of the beatitudes
Numbered. In the wind-up pattern deep

in the throat, there is nothing but creeping,
the silhouette bird moving from one segment to the next,
Numbered. In the wind-up pattern, a deep
betrayal, large green apples of the text.

Moving from one segment to the next,
avoiding their System, in plain sight I hide
from their betrayal, large green apples of the text
seen only from their underside

and avoiding their System, in plain sight I hide
as more branches are cranked into place;
obese green diners seen only from their underside,
I hear the scuffle and the bracing

as more branches are cranked into place
and triangle leaves are mobbing the Branch.

The green diners, I hear their scuffle and the bracing
as the powder blue dust goes off, I am drenched

by now. Above, a spinning manhole cover, inscribed with Beauty,
a series of explosions to the tunnel of morning,
and then a black doorway attached to a beatitude:
oval, bullet, blossom, black petal, portal of mourning.

Through the # sign at the end of a long
Branch, on the crushed blue bird's song,
I am looking for the Entrance to Bird Song.

The Constellation of a Tree Branch

The constellation of the tree branch
appears each spring above the mud of the world.

Its diamond tip touches down upon the concentric
circles. The tip is pure song and painful to hear.

The purity is needed to invoke the smaller, organic
sounds in little black vines from the mud. Only

a triangular lark can navigate the branch.
Hard cup-like yellow flowers develop on the damp

wood during the centuries it takes to come down to earth,
thick pads of lichen on the crook of the ancient creature.

The flowers listen to something the flat moon and the cold suns
hear—a trickling sound and a sensation of mist

and of not being sure is the best interpretation.
In early April, the branch makes a test run,

the bayonet tip touches down, a black line runs through the dawn,
a bassoon through the rainbow of a test strip

onto which an orchard is rapidly printed
the same three or four colors used by the printer

in the review of the rite, yellowed newsprint
where a pink blossoming haiku has been written,

a newspaper account rolling like credits.

The Cherry Blossoms Were

The cherry blossoms were clip-ons
　　much like the professions lying on the glass tray
passed around, definitions, a logic tree, the tray full of whorls
like the pond with the few iron cattails, grab them as we pass
used to shift the scene while we play music backwards:
we are used to play music on some scratched-up sticky table-surface.
The leaves were leathery, binders that fly at you
get in your face, holding the professions, & boy and girl pins,
　　& life spans
on the tray made of sea glass, lake glass, glass
of the unconscious design, the waiter holding the tray persistent
the pink pronouns.

The double names, the blossoms that are vinyl
rustle in the drawing of the breeze, data squares are in the tree
institutional-green Post-its, prayer flags (made in China??)
drift through the branches. Sometimes the road
is also caught up in the tree, an asphalt and yellow-striped
snarl mixed up with its ditch and spriggy trees-along-the-road.
The waiting man makes us drink the amniotic ink, the putrefaction
　　of our twin
self, our whole self, and then he hole-punches us
The glasses are fluted, with pinchers. Vises grip the mouth.
The daylight is inquisition. Later, bird song was distributed
throughout the tree & plastic cherries, twins.

I sent you the tree with attachments, did you get it?
Tree on a stage, tree drawn on the back wall of a cafeteria

the back wall of a story, the lining of a poem
on its sky-blue tissue paper, the Orchard of Angles
in blank blue weather. After the Cherry-Pink Rectangles Festival.
The files look like three boards, remnants of a tree house.
Cathartic, epiphany, which is a word we learned today in
      Ms. S's class.
Health Class, What did you learn about *your* family.

Lid to the Shadow

The lid to the shadow
on the path
is propped open
with an equally opaque line:
this is how many epics begin
and a male voice is singing below.
Little wind-up notes waft up on cooking smells,
then with the thinnest wisp
of a journey.
                    I'm not sure how many lines go on
below, but I'm almost at the mid-point
of my life and don't have time for beached holes,
mats and ohms, puddles peeling upward
like one-dollar Fortune Fish.
All night, my left foot wrapped in its sheepskin cloak
keeps plunging into holes.

                    He seems to be singing titles that begin with
"F." He seems to be moving around large sounds like boxes,
and a trident appears from the hole,
impaling a passing lemonic bird,
descends with the bird, adds it to the song.
The cooking smells
are becoming great swells.
Blue cloth flames flutter from the hole,
we are setting sail.

Invoice

At dusk, after a whole day at the graveyard,
the poem on my easel wasn't going so well
which is why I wrote, *The poem on my easel isn't
going so well.*

The three large disks
employed to keep dusk over the graveyard
kept falling off, denting the rental cypress,
the ponies covered in white sheets
were growing restless, and the other trees inside their costumes
were growing something worse than restless.
I'd become near-sighted from peering so far ahead.

I'd left my car keys, each shaped like a person
I know, in the wire baskets of shrubbery
at the entrance of the holy ground,
baskets for the safe-keeping of being,
and the keys had grown enormous, counts and giantesses,

and my friend Virgil was leaving more irritated
messages on my cell phone. Maybe he wanted to talk
about how after "safe-keeping"
I'd heard a scraping sound as my mentor—the first
    I'd heard of him—
pushed back a pine-green plastic lawn chair
and got up to leave, slipping down the backside
of this description in his Italian loafers,

or maybe he wants to make plans for tonight's
party in which we would throw cells at a stick.
I kept writing, but whatever it was, it kept slipping off,
slick and blank.

Those weren't sheets on the Being
of the ponies but a noxious white paint,
white-out, maybe, certainly toxic
and the blue clouds would probably always carry around
a few senseless marks that do not match
up to anything on the ground.
The white-out ponies that had grazed between gaps
in graves had long gone home.
I decided to stick it to the commanders,
Give them an invoice instead of a poem,
put ledger clouds on it, and call it "The Blur."

Flowers with Wicks

The packaging on the baby's wipes said *calming*
in gold Cyrillic font, 14 point, I believe, and it's true
I immediately sat down on the staircase and caused
it to release the final of its hysterical notes
and instead a huge tortoise-shell comb called *Goody*
replaced it, joining the two floors of the house.
It's true that I felt better, as though different scented rooms
had been slipped behind me, including the lighthouse-scented
room, the tree-house scented room, cupola-and-spiral-stair
    case-room,
not to mention window-seat scented room, splash-of-cathedral-
    ceiling-room,
and all the other rooms in brochures,
and my shadow would be made from card stock
always in the shape of a lily
lily with the tiger removed, peace Lily.

Lavender was to make me a more restful creature for others.
No longer would I pummel the pink pistons
of my fists at the dirty puddle on the ceiling
with its dingy string just asking to be pulled
as a vague, eight-foot tall figure of steam
tended over me, having inserted me into a claw
foot bath tub in a purple room in the model
of the dollhouse left on the front porch
ceiling painted as a blue sky.
No longer would I vomit my letters on the welcome mat
before the entrance to every person.

No longer would I pull at or cause the brown tag
coming out of the side of the child
who is thinking of her parents' argument.
No longer would I say awful banners about the personage of steam,
all of those words xxxxxxx'd out here,
as floral patterns are splashed around my round neck
& shoulders.

I would wrap myself in the white folio
of the plant. The room is always warm & well-lit behind me.
White-hot, actually.
Flowers with wicks, a place that spills.
I'd think of different shapes to inflate in the tub
such as 6 AM fast-walkers, the man of denim carrying a lunch pail
or the ambiguous child walking her animal-shaped trees.
Flowers with wicks in a place that spills,
& some flowers have shadows of steam
with certain words in gold cursive: I'd ignore that.
In this place that spills, I'd be the human bell inside the white folds,
the clink, flower with the play bead.

Tap, Tap, Tap

What's with this puddle that appears on a plank
in my dreams? The plank of dreaming
continuously moving, like installing
a moving walk at a major airport
only with the pattern of an elongated fingerprint
that goes on and on, a limit all stretched out
in a funhouse mirror in which case
the path is dreaming and the river is still.

This comma-shaped puddle,
a thought freed from its head,
a continent that doesn't know it exists,
murky like a piece of jade,
then back to gelatinous and gray:
It quivers at my approaching Tic-Tac-Toe boot steps
tries arranging its nerve cells to cast a menacing look
before turning a murky jade to conceal itself
in which case the path is dreaming
and the river is still.

I put my hand in, dressed in its puppet of a transit train:
"It's like helping an animal give birth,"
"It's like seeking counsel from a therapist
named Dr. Sturm" drift around in the first floor
and then X *plus* Y, *the trees are watching the river dreaming,*
and a few floors below, the scissors of the air.
On the mezzanine, I find I am afraid of hair dressers,

along with the arrow-shaped room, and right behind
What about snow globes: still waiting for the Drang
at the penthouse level is the friend-shaped shadow

who leans in from the top of the puddle,
a wallpaper of stretched-out clouds moving
behind him. He is carrying a crow bar,
a drop of venom. I squint my muscles.
I pull my act together. He is carrying a black pom-pom
in his beak, one of the three black raindrops
that drew me over fields of blank voice
to the plank across my dreams.

The Gift

Like a spittle of aluminum, a crest of fear
in a long-faced mirror, like water rushing over a box,
like a dried sentence flying in the air,
like being shown a picture of a perforated wave,
like a mark that appears on each moment,
like knowing a man is in the box,
ingot of man, and the water is shiny, highly intuitive.

Like a mote dripping with silver,
a cataract painted with lead, a sentence of gleam
and the sky speeded up, cloudy, obscure, occluded, unheard of
using a cat's eye for a planet,
like the water now almost reaching
the help desk across the marbled floor
of the enormous lobby of the hospital.
The sculpture, a prototype, donated by the major
auto-pharmaceutical industries, Spanish moss fills the ceiling
in the car port, vaults rush past picking up no one
and souls like aphids stream the stalks of the escalator.

In this gift—a sheen, a shining—wrapped around
a grid of major research hospitals in one block,
on an acre with a drop-away floor,
the mesh bow, car-sized, is heavier than it looks.
Shreds of people, the day torn off, and the incinerator is working.
Oh, dollop of man. Replica of Rodin's thinker from the gift shop,
I spot that, neon yellow teddy bear inside stalks of cellophane

for the sick child, I spot that. A man is inside the box
of cascading water. He is always wrapped in the present
moment. By now, the silvery water runs over the lines /
of this poem. I feel like shaking for the jet, the cross inside the box.
We are all headed home.

Tarot

All of this is stored on one side of the card
like covered furniture,
like summer furniture in a round room
and a portrait in a bright yellow
frame is resting on the floor:
a covered bridge, some mountains under a drop cloth,
a blank voice and a flight of concrete stairs
dropped off in the middle of nowhere,
a chipped orchard
and an M walking toward you.
It props up a portrait of a continent,
portrait of a peninsula
in a day-glo frame,
and all of this moves closer together
steps closer to the horsehair couch,
the wicker swan in a comparison,
portrait of a nephew set on the floor
to make room for a recent addition:
a long quote from a stone poem, a video clip
from five minutes ago
in which I am standing under a blossoming orchard,
which is like being shown a picture of the youngest wave.
A cherry-pink border goes around the card,
an apple-red line at 5 mph
is an arbor to the other side
of the card that is a glossy sky:
an arbor brought inside from the view
to be stored with the resort hotel
that's under a white blanket, the sand castle,
the border of square mountains.

Wild flower & Wildflower

What a lovely wildflower off in the distance over
on that side of the blank hill, don't you agree?
The one that's liver colored, or the color of dried blood,
that's basically two halves on a stick,
a sort of rusting signal flag that's still
gesturing for your attention in a day cleared out
that at times will grab onto a smoke screen
and with an elegant toss wear it as a shawl of dusk around the neck.
Like the beautiful letter you recently wrote me
in cuneiform.

The way orchids really look like vital organs on a stick
it's probably semi-precious. It's probably the last
goal of some collector with mesh for knees,
the one he'll get down on his knees to kiss
in the way all words with self need a metal hyphen
a longer idea to attach to. The wild flower

likes best to find a pocket of craving to build over,
a sort of yellow excavation. The rest can be ordinary sand
with small rocks thrown in, a few cast-die machines okay, too.
The closer we get, the more I realize it's actual
ly two ponds struggling together, the flapping sound
as they hit the blank which apparently has a surface
like a hard gymnasium floor, two ponds stapled together
and memorized. What did you use for ink?
And how did you get the paper to be so yellowed

by the time it reached me? Just as we decide to increase
our pace to approach the wild flower, I glance to the left &
see a whole field of wild things, as well as the halves
of things, in rusting plaid & soul solids, blowing in.

How About Daphne

At 40, I peel away the first layer
of bark where grey and kidney-bean red rings
of my addictions move like inner tubes down a conveyor
belt. I strip off the next layer and hold it to the light:
something I've thought over for a long time now,
like inner tubes going down a sacred river...
It would make an excellent plank, replacement pier, or ledge.
I am feeling really good...*like inner tubes going down a
    sacred river...*
I'm headed right down to the girlwood,
cinnamon-colored, to the ballpoint worm trails, to a diary
    entry from 1984:
I might even go for the moment when a branch first appeared
    on my neck.
This poise of branches is now just a purse of branches,
mostly Dog and Cat Pose. Ovid said my "face was lost in
    the canopy,"
but I'm ready to set the god of green on fire... *release him down
    the elongated river.*
Watch out. I'm ready to be a javelin, a splinter in the shadow,
    or Emily's blood-filled dash.
I'm ready to be ironwood, ready to be with the river, thriving in
    the river.

Green fires

Through the thick parts of spring
through mind-blue early morning
through the wooden pieces of a question
and the clear plastic hour with pink trees, 1:32 PM,
a black string runs through it
through the viscous landscape
and the exact moment spring begins this year
through the tipping point of a landscape
as seen through a crow's eye
buttresses and branches in a clear hour
a black runway, black recording
runs through it
thru, thru, thru

Through Louisville, KY,
through general motors, foods, electric
through the canisters and boxes of an American city
through the taxi driver, the prefixes, &, trans-
and rosy intra- on buildings, through the arrow that replaces
a letter, a black string runs through it,
through the taxi driver who looks singed
through a palimpsest of drawl over Urdu
pulling away from the sandstone
curb, saying spring starts today at 1:32 PM,
the curb lined with business men and women
Buddhas to be destroyed by the crank of an arm
to the year in which flowers appeared along my arm
I have no idea why I keep tuliping
through the buttresses and the twigs
through the tipping point of a landscape
thru

White Orchard

White blossoms seven of them along a stick,
White blossoms flowers on fire along a branch.

The names of the days but new ones turn toward me,
Diamonds of morning one by one turned on.

I am on fire from the waist up I am a flash, a glare
As a person who wears a mirror for a shirt in the blinds of the day.

If it turns out I've written these words for nobody.
If the orchard is on fire for no reason.

If it turns out I've written these words for nobody.
Along one short word, a movement.

Almond blossoms and apple blossoms. Avoid the number four
It is death in the Japanese garden.

And the backside of branches, the parts not meant to be viewed,
For then the reverse is also true.

If it turns out I've written these words for nobody.
If the orchard is on fire for no reason.

It's not true. There you are, behind that short word
A pink shadow rising on the branch.

It is true, you are the anti-.
Without a dawn word, without then.

Oh sisters, I say to these thousands on the hill,
Help me with my pruned, contorted losing.

Orchard in a Flurry

The ladder in the blossoms, the blossoms of pronouns
the circular he-she, white almost pink
and joined by copper wire,
blossoms in the thousands
How afraid I am of further medical intrusions
my own ego, need to control, specifically
need to not need the ones who shake trees
before their time and similar other
decisions. How they climb ladders to
shake branches as they would months later for apples
not caring about the damage.
I am afraid of the pick-and-choose.
The elimination of candidates and the crates
slightly rotten, sides leaning in like old barns.
How to explain later to the one who remains
that life is unfair and cruel at times.
Watching as a ladder of 14 carat gold   like a piece of jewelry
a strangest skeleton
is with an object like tweezers set
into the Petri dish   the circle of inspection
bisects, and with each move   the ladder doubles in size
unfolding at the waist
Shaking the trees, causing the flurry into nothingness.
The ladder that would grow into a staircase covered with toys
The ladder either left-handed
or oblivious. The ladder seeing the ladder
Later, seeing the ladder
leaning against the bottom of the tree

covered in huge circles of lichen
uncomfortable as a too-high lace collar
The ladder back on the ground.

Flip Book

Deep in the deck of days
after the one covered with a protective
mesh, after the seven
with the same image running through them
like a stone wall
like an emergency broadcast transmission
to a clear-blue Tuesday, after the lavender butterfly clock
across the blank field—

the dot that begins,
a flower without petals,
candle without wick,
name without stem,
flowering dot
over the orchard door.

Deep in the stack of days
before the Card of Sky
before the rainbow wall running through seven days,
before the test strip,
before the porcelain bird,
the memory that goes by
with flowers imprinted on its wings,
the meter is spinning
in names without days
between blank banks,
but long before the hour that stopped growing

and the card with a black rim,
the orchard door
covered in mesh,
bullet over
the flowering door,
the Private Entrance,
a glyph
like a cedilla in French
or ogonek in Polish
generating more material
- a person.

Grove

The prongs of the tree
hold up a white cloud
of blossoms, dim paragraph
the pewter words hold up the
splendor of a poem
the square swan
holds up cards of meaning
and after six damaged sentences
in a row, a constellation
holds up lacquered trays
of metal blossoms.
In his study, a man
walks among trees, passes
the bulleted list in the orchard
the constellation
and the oxidized tree
that has caught a pink cloud,
he picks up one announcement, some lines
are tangled together and sleeping
high in the boughs of the dedication
having chosen not to settle into
the delicate brackets
of clauses in the policy
he himself screwed into
place, this Atlas insurance,
and he puts them back
without disturbing the young
near a square cloud

with black stitching
around a name
and a proclamation
lifted overhead
like a snowy roof.

White Shadows

Acquiring an answer, rejecting the blurred shapes
the white shadows are moving under the bare tree
and so are not cast by the scissoring leaves
that elsewhere have made dotted-line objects
and constellations of family, a white drawing of a portmanteau
covered with travel stickers, someone else's, someone else's lap dog
and a figure of an uncle
        —that elsewhere have dispersed genealogies.

The shadows are from a white lake left on a floor in a rented room
and not the silent pile of the cries of other
leaves, and they reject the blurry shapes with handles,
the often xeroxed voices that surround the Ex Libris
oak growing in the middle of the library reading room,
the tree that is a roman numeral,
then a Roman soldier, as well as the sycamore
that becomes a German soldier, in Fraktur.

Highly intuitive
        a silver spill
comes from under the door frame of the rented room
with the lake in the middle of the floor
and it knows something
about the clusters of seeds that drag themselves
over linoleum fields
back to their tree of origins
in a slow, death-defying rattle of skin tones,

knows because there are the black shadows not cast by anything
and it knows something about the shadowless place with only a tree.

It knows something about the figure of a man
who wears a lid of shadow for a hat
while a caw spreads on the ground,
the man who a moment ago had been stretched out
on the bony ground under the tree
who now, as the silver spill approaches
with its pictures, has been traveling by foot for days
to return to his twenty-six armed tree,
who pretends to doze against the pewter rock wall
his face in a lid of shadow and an exaggerated hayseed
springing from his mouth as though on a pole
and he waits for me to return down the lane
as the cries of the shadows become louder,
as the silvery spill moves across the glossy thunderstorm,
the flash card of the sky that will leave
more answers lying on the ground.

Oh, white shadows of omission,
white shadows that have protected for so long,
you raise up your pyramid of salt and blind sand,
pyramid turning into a man with a name,
and in this place where I outlast him,
you hoist three white leaves of soul, age, experience
on a palm tree on the trumpeting panels
of preexisting dawn.

After the Cherry Festival

Mass-produced answers are rolling gently in rollers of warm breeze
along with pink, green, and yellow threads of pollen,
fuzz from the plaid of spring, lint from the silly plants
in the cracks of the parking lots, along the curb,
and yellow road lines are making the ground a Chanel suit.
Mass-produced answers in the warm breeze end up under trees
that end up planted in dividers at the mall, under the elephant-gray
     feet,
banging up against the rinds of exhaust-soaked soil
in the rolls of breeze. Tickets to the cherry blossom festival,
these answers rapidly printed, the 2-3 colors overlap on the stubs,
so different from the easel
I fumble at in my pocket, setting up a triptych
representing the tree, "After the Cherry-Pink Rectangles Festival"
in blank blue weather. It takes three panels for me
to get close to the tree —taking the letter "e" out of a poem—
sometimes I just leave the stainless steel
easel empty under the tree, at the stone feet in yellow sandals.
Mass-produced answers rolling in the rollers of the warm breeze,
From a hundred yards away, I can sense the perfume test strips
inside the windowless façade, over the sleeping backs of the sedans.
The tickets and candy wrappers for the gum that tastes like
     blossoming
haiku pink—collect the right three, and you'll have your answer.

Push-Pin

I push-pin myself
into the contact paper,
into the wallpaper on the back wall of morning,
through to the black and white graph of motherhood,
into the stack of days, the days that fly at
you or flap madly away, into a dog-eared landscape
on a virtual desk blotter. While I'm at it, I push myself
into the factoid, chapter and verse, into the pewter public notice, draft
    for a billboard
about breathing, handbill, post no handbills, and I hold up two grimy
    pot holders, Betty Crocker,
éclairs with their cold white cream as I push into a prescription for
    weather,
into the baby's cry which is a transparent shape named January, into
    a chart of how many times I've been interrupted,
and then into the adult squiggle on the audit of fear, into the kiss of
    peace allotted
by the spider priest, near the Buddha night-light. I am the push-pin
    in the two flip books of my daughters,
        in the sticker sheet of one hundred guesses given to me by a friend,
and into the pink quake, that wrinkled pink sheet,
man is but a rhythm on a stick: into that. Into a Note to Self on strictly
    mental stationary.
The head of the pin is thinking about the 1970's, so it's a sort of amber
    Pax, enclosing
a tiny girl w/ pigtails and a therefore symbol on each cheek. From
    here-on-out,
everyone will have to use the same recipe for roux, and the dead bird

wearing a veil from the blueberry-bush netting that killed it is at the
   bottom
of the stack and is Joan of Arc. Push Pin, I am a cartoon character
in a religious painting, and I hold up a steel-grey degree, the missing
   page from the findings section.
I push-pin the permit for the immolation, so that the ice shack that
   balances precariously
on the tacky metal roof of the Victorian knows about the cupola
   standing on the ground.
I can't help but notice that the garage has been dismantled,
and its shards of sentences, yardsticks, and
the floes of rooms, are in a pile beneath me, with a note that says
   (to me), forget it.

Serrated Tree

Some branches weighted more than others
will trigger reactions. The powder blue ones,
for instance, do not really lead to the orange ones;
Person A complains to Person C about Person B behind
B's back. The branches are color-coded, with little numbers,
and you'll learn to avoid the underlined parts
as the squirrels do while carrying their trumped-up tails
                                        walking down the hair-pin
on the balls of their feet, sometimes chanting as they run along
        the edge
tossing chewed-up letters over their shoulders.
Their tree-shaped screw-on butt plumes
are the inverse
                        of the bolts
that occasionally go straight to the ground, a series of jagged steps
that grows only on the right side of a tree, the icy set of stairs
                                        that leads straight down
to the basement of the matter, a zap
pow!-ing at the tail-end of a sentence
that causes a crash that rocks the image
of the tree back and forth
silently, followed by an icy blank you'll feel in your temples.
Person D leaving the table and walking straight into the night.
From my house, more little blue houses
hanging from a birch.

Houses with Shadows

I.

The shadows are taped on the houses:
loosely, they rise and fall in
the measure of the summer breeze
on the faces with strong features
which include the following:
widow's walks, dormers,
strong cleft chins, stately federalist
with widow's peak, a four-square
with box hedges, crisp pin-striped
siding and French doors, opened, listening
to a daughter's harpsichord recital.
Seven houses are founding fathers
on the bright village green
two wearing their crosses in different ways,
sideburns of cypress and brass rules
for banisters, so unlike the bank converted
into one of the new denominations w/ drive-up
window and father-daughter dance
in teen lock-in, metal fold-up chairs,
replacing % sign for the most recent interest rate.
The one woman is in the back
the coils of her hair being repaved,
her high collar stiff, an all-white apple tree,
on which is pinned a cameo
appearance in which a figure every
five seconds does a mad jig
though she doesn't ever say anything. Ever.

2.

...

Follow directions.
Follow the scissors in the sky,

mauve-handled,
moving around the perforated trees
and the floating text box.

The landscaper,
he drew in every leaf

with the handle of the shears.
His glue gun
is visible under a pile of bark mulch,

he is gone for the day.

Plastic bins for his categories,
beads, seed pearls, clasps

and marbles.
Loosely, the shadows will rise and fall

in the breeze across the strong geometry

of the houses.

3.

A daughter is pinned to the lawn,
to the bright village green w/
large, stiff trees and croquet mallets,
a cannon with two balls
and shadows not cast from anything
anybody is playing.
The sounding of a Paul Revere bell
over a crocheted gazebo,
the town, incorporated in.
Near this coupon for the historical society
a man in an overcoat cut
from a mystery, whodunit,
walks off in a halo of yellowed paper,
passing the gazebo from a book of confessional poetry.
His back always to us;
he carries a sledgehammer
makes a diagonal on the field
leaves to report to
the white churches carved from a single
flake of lead paint
about to crumble in.
"A girl abducted by a robin."
There goes the robin with a tomato-orange
oval on his t-shirt from Target
carrying in his beak the paper doll,
one arm struggling feebly.
A daughter is pinned to the lawn.
This is how the daughter makes love now,
see the twin blades of the legs.
A black heart, a shadow on the ground.
I don't need to look down;
Someone is muttering "mother of –"
I can feel the spot on my chest darkening.

Candle Holder Holding It Together

The circle of friends—are five men in iambic clay
pentameter on a table at a restaurant always threatening fore
closure. Five people—who are mostly hands,
stay together because they are hyphenated.

The circle of friends—shiny chests that sing
—are technical computer software so dial to speak
are birds with cuff links—who rest in yoga trees
and work for BAE, a TM flame at their center,

woven flame near the Thich Nhat Hanh napkin holder.
They meet. At a crowded restaurant always threatening ex
tinction, and serving Chilean sea bass—meet at the corners
of a season or at solstice, after time hiding in a pottery barn

at the end of one long pier. With merlot-scented candle at center,
with shiraz-scented candle at center, with many sparkling feats,
five friends in turn surrounded by 5 men, who-put-their-hands-
together-in-prayer—when Figure 1 rises from his crouch

to use the restroom. Fig. 2, a dentist by training,
waits two minutes, then crosses the wire of a border
set along the length of the busy bar. Figs. 3 and 4
notice the snow flake outside policing the stars.

Fig. 5—holds on. While the horizon is downloading,
the myth on the tag says people rise
from adobe tops, causing the dawn as well
as the pattern on the blankets.

Sung

What they said broke off and fell to their feet
in a clean break at the lips, snapping like a handle from pottery.
It might have been a psalm, a mantra, or something read off a label.
It joined a song with a clean hole in it on the ground
littered with hub caps and fenders, dented mouthpieces,
pipes and stems, insertions for beaks, a yellowed ditty.
Then a sparrow with a black ribbon around its neck hobbled
on one leg to peck at it among needles for the sacred transmission
of hormones, and a caption that stepped backward,
deleting itself.
                              From across the orchard of parking
comes a mother-and-daughter team. Can we take
 what we want. Of course, this is an all-you-can-eat pick-yr-own,
but stay between the apostrophes. Between the apostrophes
the eating is good. A good day is a cheap day
beneath the sky of banners, clouds shoving them
selves back inside the long necks of chimneys.
At the office we have a hundred of these;
 the engineers jam them in a closet. It's funny how but yet
even as I pick, I think of the circle of friends
their shiny purple chests, cuff links and the lips of birds,
that a cappella group and the warning they had sung at the office.
At the office, first a layer of shopping bags was discovered
rolling of its own accord
under the floorboards
then a hundred clay soldiers.

The Therapist to the Explorer,

The green secretions of woods
The fringes of the woods, the drawn-out
vegetation of anticipation
the moss vines ivy dripping over things
The green signs that flap against one
in large wet sheets, the pulses.

You say there were also messages printed on logs
from your predecessors as well as immediate supervisor
that one place was stapled to the next,
that one branch was the creature called an alligator, &
that an animal head lived on a torso with britches
another, knee-highs, in what we now call Virginia?
and that the waterfall spoke to you on that tinsel cliff, something
you'd now like to remember?

Pyrrhic Victory

All of my wings pulled out and stacked in the corner
like old tires, like a pile of old cells
which are trash can lids held to dawn
red or blue rimmed, those shields
Because my mother has fallen.
And above her is a zigzag, no, a skid.

Asphodel

I.

My desk has been brought down to Hell,
an OFM Metal Desk, Marvel Series C 71,
and in the backyard, a few of the trees are symbolic,
taken directly from Tarot cards
along with the pewter rock wall, seven pentacles.
It was fortunate that I'd cleared out my desk
though in one drawer, three Pisces paper clips
wait like primitive fish poised to walk on land
and the beige drawer seems vast to them, stadium-sized.
                    ... My stoic little desk
that wishes now it were a credenza with hand-carved
drop front in cherry, or a Teacher's Desk with Center Drawer
or one of the FM Secretarial Series with Right Return,
stands with four feet in Hell on the floes of rooms
that surf the magma of non-stop change
while as of yet none of the figures cast about
in the world-sized field have noticed it.

II.

Was it because of evolution? I doubt it.
Because of the contents of the lilac folder?

Waning crescent and waxing gibbous moons
are left by the weight of my desk in the petals

of the wall-to-wall carpet that's like a crowd of bland people.
A hope chest of Revere pans and ramekins,
a treasure chest making the sign for secret above its heart
could have stood here—it's about the same length—
something that needn't have removed itself but did.

Hold on a minute.
I just received information that my sofa has been taken
    to the cliff of the unfinished,
                and it balances there like a sedan.
The one that matched
    the sectional and the love seat all for $799 and the sangria,
right over the orange & brown streaks of Indian paint brush.

In my desk's window,
the Tarot trees are arranged in a baseball diamond
with the family oak and the Norwegian pines,
who were already quite morose, and a caw spreads on the ground.
A Roman numeral centers itself over a sleeping man.
I am pretty certain they'll be using my head as their baseball.

tiny low garden

the tiny low garden in fine print
grows by repeating itself, the contractual maze:
there's a wait as though beside a blinking cursor
a bush with tea roses of sunlight
can happen twice in a row. I wake up and can tell
it will be a hot one. I raise my eyelids which are gritty tents
half-way up, careful not to disturb the purple mass
to my side that I have literally moved mountains for. Already off in
the middle distance where the mountains have been scraped away
in the middle no longer with mountains, the mountain-less distance
people in catering uniforms are setting up the hedges
for the event in the garden. It's amazing how fast
the green bramble of vows throws itself on top of
compliancy. The entire screen occasionally flickers;
that doesn't surprise me as somewhere to the left
an indelible civilization is a mega-drain on resources.
I like the secrecy of my fringes, swish, elaborately long on the tents
and the watching of them without them knowing I am watching.
Six or seven inches longer than they have to be.
Now come the white dishes which clatter, the calla lilies
(of course this would be that bride's wish). Mesh of planning
that inadvertently catches a few birds thinking those are real berries.
I guess it's fair to say that the wine critic is only a twisted tree in the
corner. A Timex?? Others appear to enjoy the contractual maze.
It is admirable how much fine print can be fit
into a narrow band daylight flirting in the cursive,
topped by gritty pearls in the morning
that is formatted on a small screen with thick black margins,
a picture frame balanced at the edge of a working stove.

Napkin-Folding Instructions

The Bird of Paradise Napkin Fold
The Basic Silverware Punch Fold and The Diamond
The Pyramid Napkin and the Arrow
The Bishop's Hat, the Rose, the Sail

from the napkin guide, for the word of the day
at Merriam Webster's, slumgullion, on a plate
of restaurant review. If you burn the soup
he is a regular chawbacon, shouts at the staff in vulgate,
but serves up a spoony kickshaw,
gewgaw of two pom-poms of ice cream with gold tinsels
that he portly watches from the kitchen portal
matching match.com couples bend to eat, in Modern Lighting
napkins fly behind him around the kitchen, brassy cawing?

Not to mention how to fold a shirt, a flag, a
Handkerchief mouse,
and the fitted sheet.
Turn any meal into a festive occasion just by the way you fold.
YouTube will show how-to, making an Elephant or Bunny
Towel. A napkin doesn't just rest on the table. It is a personality,
says Milliken Napery.
Even one that looks like a necktie across the plate, at the
        lay-off dinner,
From Latin *mappa*, For oryoki

Pinprick

With swords rented from the library
these figures in robes with untoward
    and pewter hair,
they will whipsaw the froward,
logging off, they cut through space
cutting white space into parenthetical cubicles
rendering the texture of listening
into references, saying I can't help myself
and, which number did you pull?
With numbered swords
and with numbered words (5,246), tiny numbers on the hilts
of their phrases and on wires, they fly at you
on the prow of punishment
on the cathedral ceiling
of the reading room
& far below is the tiny head of the
reference librarian. The first line of this poem is a footnote /
and in lower case, part of the poetic subterranean, /
I say, and not meant to be used in this way. /
The angels with numbered phrases
are at the Dewey decimals and quickly going lower,
a bouquet of numbers that makes a sawing sound.
Are you wikipedia? The numbers on the swords
Swizzle sticks, stir stick, incense, ju-ju, Pez dispensers
are as small as footnotes. *They* are small footnotes
oh, Academia, onward.

Google Books Brothers

We are lying on our backs
in the grammar handbook looking up
at paragraphs standing in for clouds

some as long as the subtitle
16th edition, dragging Christmas-red ribbons.
One cloud is several lines long

and uses descriptive technique from Hanley's
Guide to Authorship with Gradual Steps
Toward Grammar which takes using italics

and giving the author's last name.
The cloud exhales and tows ribbons
over an exhortation about farming practices

and tickles. We lie on the deck
of the steam ship lil' bro
drew in our father's calf-skin collected

Aldridge, where a horse and buggy
are also parked. My literary brother
provided a sketch of blossoming chicory

for the roan, (Sally, the mare
our father bought from Smithy), invoice

slipped now into the book, smoke-house

construction costs too. We also appear
in the frontispiece of the *Customs
House,* and on the ginger hill

where we played the Whip all
afternoon long, blonde hill the color
of my favorite girl's head &

were given a whup'n after supper
and were not given licorice whip
Mary Jane, Swedish fish, root beer

barrels, conversation hearts, or Pop Rocks.
And I drew this kid brother
 into Google Books where he floats

electronically, wearing his head gear as
well as his mouth guard, scanned
upside-down in his breeches.

New-Fangled Greeting Card

rubies along the shore
garnets along the shore

of the cardboard lake

the word *sure* is semiprecious
and included in a promise of a visit

which will surely involve their wine-in-a-box

which, when never happens on time or soon enough
is like the missing stone
in the gate
from the World's Fair tiara, 1958

The greeting card startles the old lady
with an oil spill of yellow and red
a manic sun serenades her
by electric guitar

on her M.F.K. Fisher dock
with oysters bienvenue in a jar
the pine-needles-as-rosemary
falling onto exquisite bread from Harvey's
Apparently, the old lady dumped the contents of her jewelry box

along the shore
so the family starts in wading
through the box turtles, Tiffany water bugs
and a lake shore that turns out to be pasteboard

not too far off a marsh is drawn in,
and Merlot Creek

frilly black and white water
to be colored in with the enclosed tiny karma sutra brush

The Form

Where have all the questions gone?
Just an intuitive sense of what's being asked
Telephone poles with tufts at the top, a dotted line road.
A few seconds after she wakes, the form appears

as a dotted line road emerging from her head. Each day asked
to fill the form out again. To be one's own official
no one in sight, all her friends gone to the shore.
Strange shore, for those who never took a vacation,

lapping at nothing. To be the only official
hefting facts and numbers into place in the blanks
along the side of the road that is vacant,
each answer a pile of yellowed blocks turning,

the clouds are under this landscape, the billboards blank
Sometimes she doesn't receive the phone call for weeks.
The words change with heavy clunks, she turns
On this cloud that smells of urine that her husband

died in. She's been sleeping downstairs for weeks.
To be a young woman again, walking to the well, asked
for her thoughts. Up ahead, a figure is walking the line, his
form familiar, a repair man with a cinched waist who appears

too far off to hear what she says, no matter what she asks.
No matter, she suddenly feels like flirting and moves down the road.
A few more palm trees and a pelican appear.
The pelican changes into a heron. The form ends. She starts over, or it is gone.

Inversion

The black bead of the searcher
is bird-shaped in the lined park
not on a lyre but on the wires
of the park the birds invert song
their toes clipped to the wires
sending it back down to the red playground
as a column of black bubbles
in a form that needs to be filled out
in a many-lined search.

The song inverts the birds
the clips of their toes on the wires
on the remaining enamel of the sky
one by 1 the words bend back
and forth on these live lines
in the yellow lined cloud
that is passing my way
while the song is inverting the birds
of the park, they rise to serve
Petri dishes of petal-pink
rickety watch towers, spring moon
compressed plum song
where the sky peters out.

Where the sky peters out
the black bead of the seeker
now on alert another hunter a bead
on the horizon that bounces
that twangs with every movement.

Wicker park

Background and foreground are woven together
and faces, a fracas, emerge in the weaving
with braided sentences white as a cut onion
in the clicking breeze, under the spread of the mothering tree
that's silk-screened on the brown and white sky threads
in a poem that must be completed in July.
A bleary yellow truth several stitches across, the sun,
and the huh of a lion. Can barely make them out
or tell how many men, women, and children, stems
stalks, pods, the leader is the one with the bent tip,
unless they're talking. The children use a lot of flat "w" words.
The decision is when to leave the tree,
under the pot of nightfall or the open hand of day.
When the leader speaks in braided letters
red from plant dyes, his statements rise high under the canopy
while several sonic basements below them
in the cool levels of the earth, after a descending argyle,
the family of plants waits in deeper silence.
The father wears the smallest bulb on his back.
Many protective tendrils, the veins of everyone strain
to stay quiet. Far off, to the right,
the weaving for Chicago starts, picks up metallic blues and silver,
and a man in a second-hand bookstore is leafing through
The Family of Man (in passable condition).

Sign Park

They put number signs down to avoid sitting on the mud
that's mentioned everywhere this time of year
to protect their loved ones, esp. the collie
with his addled brain who peers out from sun-bleached bangs
like an overhang of hay. Then into the mud they stick
grass and red plaid, green and blood plaid, the family
insignia, which in August would seem like slash mark wild
flowers in grassy parallels. They choose a tree that's all lumps
to sit collectively under & unpack
      hundreds of plastic trays, then unseal
their unusual collection of hors d'oeuvres.
The women wear sacking with swatches of Burberry (knock-offs)
the men in games of argument raise what look like golf clubs
      painted Chinese
red, the women raise the stakes with parasols of buttercups or
      grass stains.
In another setting, this is called menschärglichnicht.
Hark, hee, and hah—in general, they use a lot of "h" words.
Across the park in a filled-in oblong, shirtless college boys like
      fish gulp at
Frisbees. Every fifteen seconds, the collie's effort to not add
his variable to their set reaches maximum exertion. Meanwhile,
across the swampy soccer field, the goalpost fast-walks
to the Roman Porta-Potties. And one group is minus two,
a plus sign, love-colored, floats near a woman's elbow,
floral dress. The man's arm, thatched. While on the plot
      underneath them
the new things of spring sprout blindingly white, cross hook.
The collie bolts off down the hill,
finally noticing what it is in the grassy parallels.

public poem

A white sentence in all caps
A block letter sentence
A Property Of, above the greening sink
That's really, an oxidizing rose.
A primrose from the dunes
Is a corsage to be worn by the public restroom.

A 1980's sentence spray-painted gold
In careful Pristina,
Oh, poor Richard, next to Showcard Gothic
And Playbill but far away from Rod.
Platinus eats corn the long way
In Latin high on the lavatory wall
Near the convention center.

On a Buddhist hum
A tunneling attached to the inflatable funhouse
That turns out to be birth. No Shoes.
The Dalai Lama is speaking tonite at the Nike-Citibank
Convention Center. The bodies of cars will be parked tight
Next to the Coliseum Grill-Bar.

You poets are all a bit daft in the head.
And further, adds Plato to Ion,
Your mother a feminine ending, # sign, three exclama-
Tion points.
Rhetorica ad Herennium, the oldest surviving

Handbook on writing, advises us to not use
Figurative language, circa
84 BCE. To do so will make the body of your prose
Flatulent, false, effeminate.

It's been over an hour since a stall door
Last slammed.
It's been several seconds
Since anything's been mentioned in the poem
And yet it's still running.

To the Tune of
"The Constellation of a Tree Branch"

Waiters in orange robes shimmy up the bent bough of spring
to deliver compressed plum song,
squeezing past their boss, the zodiac.
It is the Year of the Dog,
the watchtowers of moonlight are rickety,
and more branches are cranked into place.